Ndilapa Nkosi

by

orde

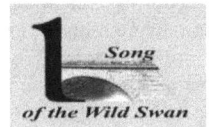

Published by Song, 2014.
Song is an Imprint of:
Song of the Wild Swan Ltd.
1 Folly Bridge, Oxford, OX1 4LB, UK.
www.songwildswan.com
tel +44 (0) 1865 240572
fax +44 (0) 1865 246565
e: info@songwildswan.com

Ndilapa Nkosi
ISBN 9781909777125

First published: 1979, Private printing, (6 copies).
Second Publication 1981, Ororey Publications, Cape Town, 200 copies.
eBook and Book: 2014 Song, Oxford.

Acknowledgements

Song eBook Design series by Laurence Hutton-Smith.
Cover Design: Laurence Hutton-Smith.
Cover Image: Text from Ndilapa Nkosi, © orde, Oxford, 2014.
Book production: Amaury Marinho Junior

Contents

Provenance

'Lcs demoiselles d'Avignon ont déjà trenre-trois longues années de rente'
Lc désir attrapé par le queue, Pablo Picasso, 14 January 1941.

How ironic that I am sitting some thirty years later and thinking about the e-book publication of this lyrical comedy, written under the hammer blows of feeling and intensity at the time. Has my soul and its muse being novacained since writing it? Probably. Perhaps before – even.

At that time I was on a roll, intensely and without interruption writing *Ndilapa Nkosi*, and had begun on the second and third parts of the trilogy – *Antomat, Diplony of the Orb* (an epic comedy) and *The Argonauto Vineyard* (a tragic comedy) titles which I have not altered since, whose poetic category follows the definitions of the poet Hölderlin's distinctions between lyric, epic and tragic poetry.[1] The history of Ndilapa Nkosi is short. There were other events around my life, a heavyness. I was folding. In desperation I wrote to my two literary heros at the time Etienne Leroux and Samuel Beckett via their publishers and enclosing a short Glossary/Dramatis Personae of Ndilapa Nkosi (which is reproduced in this publication) and one of the six type-written copies I had made of Ndilapa Nkosi and with a note saying '*either I am practicing gross self-deception or you must acknowledge me*'. Their wonderful replies, reproduced in this publication, were received on the same day – more irony, and on my birthday. At the time, however, I could not see their value and I even misread the question mark of Beckett as pertaining to the Dear. My state of mind! I debated destroying all my work – Etienne wrote another incredibly moving letter discouraging this but one thing led to another and I still destroyed all my work.

Just over a year later I self published *Ndilapa Nkosi* in a small run of I think it was 200 copies – the Ororey publication - in which the introduction is

---

[1] The lyric poem, idealistic in appearance, is ingenious in its meaning. It is a never-ending image of a single emotion.

The epic poem, artless in appearance, is heroic in its meaning. It is the image of great aspirations.

The tragic poem, heroic in appearance, is idealistic in its meaning. It is an image of an intellectual conception.

reproduced here as well including the cover, and back page having found one of those six type-written copies mentioned above. Some reviews followed, reproduced in this publication as well.

And that is where it has laid – although attempts to get it published in the past were not successful. I am going to start writing soon the second and third part of the trilogy anew – now called provisionally – *The Soul's Heritage.*

orde
Oxford, 4 December 2013.

Say
Something
Nomsa
Eh
Apartfiar
eh
I can say its a thing
but it is so much used to us
us
so much used to us
now
that we are used to it
but there are some other things that are hard
baas
very hard
Sometimes
you sometimes
it is difficult to make a pass
eh
passes
are the main things
passes are difficult to us because
if you leave it
maybe you forget it
at home
you are taken into the
in the
custody
yes
that is the main thing eh
and you are locked up
Yes that is the main thing is the pass
        taken into custody and you are
                locked up
even though you have gotten it at home
they

don't take you home to fetch it
I don't know what it is eh
ah what does it mean
It is to be seperated
it is to be seperated to each other
It does not matter
if if
you can mix freely
not that you
                    I
i must not enjoy
the other facilities
I want to enjoy everthing
and
I want to be free
that's the thing
I want to be free
be
to move you know
eh
because like other people
blue people
whom we like to visit sometimes
yes
because we like them
Now we can't because this
this
we there there
are hard laws
that you can't visit people whom you
                              like
the other colour
it is not good
that way
we must stay brother
brotherhoodly
yes
I think so
it is very nice like that and enjoy

                    this world
it can be like this
e
a person will own his or her place
but
then we can be friends
visiting him
like it that way tog
I think it is like that
Apartfiar
it is like that
it is good to move freely
but you can have your own place
but I am free to go to you
to go to eh
there will be no ill feelings
Eh I know that there are hooligans
who are not respecting people
who have got a horrison in their minds
those can be
locked up
I think they are the ones who should be
                    put away
to be treated there
not
to be thrown away
also to be eh to be
learnt
yes
l think that is the way in the world to
                    live in peace
it is very nice like that
I don't mean to go and take other peoples
                    things
that he has worked for
no
wah

a person must also stand up on his feet or
                        on her feet
and work for a place
a place
to buy something to buy some
to buy some land
I mean you can buy land and do what you like
                        there
l mean being a gentleman or a lady
eh and no bad things to be eh
I think that is what I   would like Apartfiar
                        to be
tog
to be on my side
.   .
you mean no uhm
Nomsa   .
No strict laws to say that you can't go there
eh
you will see
if you behave
by your behaviour
then
you are free
then you are free
to come
eh
I think it will be a nice world
.   .
why
but why what
why do you think
who do you think
but why do you think all the Safarners are
so afraid
they fear that the Greens will just take over
and
Nomsa   .
Aeach

ah
what I think is
because they ought to be
because we people
we were first bad to them
our forefathers
when I learn about
eh
that
blood river
I don't know if I am right
Isaloadof
our people started the
a
eh
those old forefathers of ours
because of their conflict together
we new people
new people
we people now
we don't know it now
now we don't even think about it now
because we are
I think we people
we are now civilised
we don't
we are some civilised people in us now
that want to stay
please
those people are barbaric ways
to kill
to dinner
you see
its
bad bad bad
we don't want it
we do understand
I understand that the root
the root

came from that
evil root
so the Safarners tries to repeat the thing
I am sure it is the
thing
If our forefathers didn't do that
it would not happen
so the children now want
revenge
to the others children
eh
I wonder if it can be just made alright now
please please tog
it is bad
it is going very far bad
and now it is other people who is suffering
because of this
a lot of people now they suffer because of that
that
blood river war
this is the cause
I can see it

.   .
Y
Nomsa   .
Ihm

.   .
Now they must allow the blue and green to
live anywhere
Nomsa   .
They can't do it
now
because it is like that
and the root
is in the blood
you see
eh
I don't think it is
right
for to

mix the
houses
now
I don't think so
they must be given
also the greens must be given a place
everything like
in a town
a eh great difference because
eh
a great difference if
you go like in the locations
onto the townships
the poor areas
you can't get places like these
you can just do that
for the time is
Ripe
the time is ripe for every nation to go
                              forward
they must allow it
I don't mean they must allow the people to
                              come
and sit and stay in
other peoples homes
their houses
I think they must have a place where they
                              can move freely
and a city
must be built
with nice houses
you see
and electricity and all the facilities
that other nations have
I think so
I am referring to a Green
a a a a
non-believer
ja

because he is not the same as them
ja
he is then for them a
a
non-believer
I mean
they can do just that for
eh
what can I say
eh
they can do just that for
for just
just to be
you know
just to be
good
to them
because they are also trying to be people
they are trying to be people
I am also one of them
I want to live in wonderful places
e
nice
and yes
to own a house
a nice house
so please tog
a nice place
a room
clean
with water
        electricity
so please tog
they must forget this
e
they must make a try
make it a nice place
also

and the
permit
pass
laws
how does it affect the family
Nomsa   .
the families
are divided
that is the thing
the father is to be here
the mother up country
and it is
dry
there
tooo dry
if they can make a nice place
like a farm
they can allow them to have these things
tog
it is better to be free
not to mix
to have to mix
there are safarners
who like these people
us people
yes
they are so much used to them
yes
they are employers
they like to come to their place
to the huts
they like to take their
they care for them
yes the blues like the greens
yes they take them to
yes they are wonderful people
good hearts

but he start
is the thing
the root
comes from the that thing
the
blood river
war
but please if it only could be forgotten
those people
those people
are people
who fought
for the thing they knew
themselves
then then then
Yes
but we people
we people
now
of today
we want to live in peace
no fear
becautse we try
we we we
they taught us to be nice people cultured
civilised
now we want to stay like that
we can't go back to
the hardships
now

.   .

now then but what about your culture
Nomsa   .
yes yes
the backgroung up country
which is now
behind the times
because
eh

the greens want to be like the blues
their clothes
.   .
but is it now nice
to wear
what you
are
wearing
don't the young
ones
want to
Nomsa   .
It is
beautiful
they do it now
they like it
differently
not like before
they used to rub
ochre ochre
they don't like the ochre now
now they just wear
this materials
like the ochre
I saw one who
was wearing
nicely
Isango
she wore
white
and with white beads
beads
oh it was wonderfully beautiful
everything
is done now in this time
everything now
it is now
it is up to date
now
so even to be allowed

to get what
we want
to buy
and
to be allowed
to have it
no
I don't mean
in the blue places
because
the blood
can't
not yet
the thing is in the blood
another
safarners
told me
it was true
it was
a congregation
they can't do otherwise
because
they were taught
this thing
was taught
when they were
like that
that the green man
is
no good
eh
what can I say
he must never
stay
next to a green man
because
those green men
at that time
were like that

but
now
they
young ones
now
they don't like this
.   .
like
what
Nomsa   .
the
seperation
too
much
eh the young people
want to know
the other people
other
cultures
other
nations
yes
these young ones
eh
they also
brought us
up
to understand
a
human being
is
a
human being
but then
we can't just come and
grab
the blue peoples
things
because they have

worked
hard
they are
the workers
of the things although
we are
they
also the people
who helped
build
this road and these buildings
but the brains are from them

.   .

but then
what about
the politics
the politics
Nomsa   .
No
politics politics
are easy
if
these things can be done
to be given
all
that the people
want
in their land
you understand
they want
politics politics
are things
our politics
its
a
a
a
its
Apartfiar
that is the politics

we know
eh
eh
eh
you see
this is the thing
which
taught
us
politics
eh
you know I mean
by taught
politics
is to know
you can't
go there
he
he'm
eh eh
so we think it is politics that
we don't
know
exactly what politics is eh

it is a lot
of laws
which say you are not allowed to
this and that
and that one
that to me
even on the road
eh
what can I say
eh eh eh
the eh
s t a i r w a y s

there is another side for us
I understand that
is
because we can't be together
I wonder
now
It is a bus stop
Yooooah
where are we
Ja
go this way
ja ja
turn turn turn
ja
please
I am sorry
this is what i think
.   .
but what about the people like
Lungisa
does he
not want everything that the blue man has
Nomsa   .
I think so
because
the young ones
want
to be as their blue brothers are
they want to be
and
for their education they want
to be allowed
to practise
For them now when the finish practise
I mean
when the finished school
they can't get
a job
they can't get
work

and practise
they can't get
places
where they can practise
I mean
the standard of their
they wanting
of their education
they have to go
and work
maybe
in the gardens
in the housekeeper
I mean
waiters
this is the thing
now
these people
now
it is nice now
when they look at
other nations
serving the public
that is right
so they want also to
do
that yes

   .   .

there are so many blue people
who are leaving   because
they feel
there will be another big battle
of blood river
Nomsa   .
Yes
they are quite right
they should think
so because
now
it is enemies

by these laws
yes
the laws the laws
if
the government
would make them nice
have have
everything
not everything
but as other people get
wiln't
be
anything
.   .

like what like what
Nomsa   .
I mean
our children
must learn and then after
learning
because they tried hard to be
what they are
after learning
now
after finishing
they must be
allowed
to practise
what they want
whatever whatever
costs
I mean
whatever
w o r k
they want to do
.   .

so no Apartfiar
then
Nomsa   .
No Apartfiar

I am coming to that then
yes
.   .
OK
then
talk about Apartfiar
how
does it affect you
why
Nomsa   .
it affects us
in
the lives
in
the daily lives
in the daily lives
we know that everything is changed
the world
now
wants love
kindness
and understanding
so much so that
we can face
the things
that are outside
but I will stress this
that
we are merely asking
a begging
to the authorities
because we
I can say we know nothing
because the blue people
taught
us all these wonders
we see
in front of us
e
but now

this is the fault
they have got the power
the government
has got the power
I understand now
that the people are
scared
of the greens
eh
taking over their
homes
because they were so
whatsaname
so oppressed
that is the thing
the laws
were so hard
but now the poe
people
think
that they
are
all dead
they are
no more
living

.   .

which people
Nomsa   .
the greens the greens
ha

.   .

they are all dead
Nomsa   .
JJJAAA
sss
they are just moving
they are shadows
I can say it

because of the hardships
because of the laws
men
are shadows
they can't say
anything
I remember when they were
hit by
kerries
he
.   .

kerries
Nomsa   .
Yes the kerries
at Agnayn
ha ha ha
.   .

the greens
were hit
by
the blues
Nomsa   .
yes
maa
it was bad
from that time
now
they are invalids
some people
they have got
they have broken
what the name
broken arms
.   .

Why
were they hit
Nomsa   .
because they started
riot
0691

they wanted the other
s
burnt
they burnt
their passbooks
because they
said
the passbooks are
their trouble
at night
the police come
although they give us they townships
to stay there
in the houses
ut they still
come
they have got a pass
but they come
and ask for it
demand it
eh
early hours of the morning
eh
they come
they say now
this thing is not good
better
burn
these things
that is why now are
invalid
.   .
and what happens if
they burn it
Nomsa   .
you can never have
a place to
stay
I mean
it is no good

not to have
the pass
but it is good to have it so
that when
you have got an accident it shows
where you are staying
that way
it is good
not to be
waat can I say
to be
chased   insdie
insdie
inside
your house
and even if you are inside
your house
they ask again
where is your pass
hey
in your house hehehehheh
that is why it is difficult
.   .
but the blue man has the
fiar
Nomsa   .
Yes
.   .
If there are no passes that
the green man
there will be
crime
all over the street
Nomsa   .
of
course
that ya
that is
true
and now

there is
no work for them
many
the pass
can
be better
a little bit
eh no
it will be like this
the
home
lands
will be developed
will be developed
a lot of work there
and farms
so that the people don't
be starving
they starve there
now
they come to the
towns
there are lots of things in the
towns
they steal there
they snatch things
eh eh
because they have nothing to
eat
nothing to eat
up country it is hard and dry drought
.   .

in the homelands
Nomsa   .
yes don't know how to irrigate
they were not taught these things
I mean I know
they are a whole lot of them
who don't want to go to schoool
it is

easy
the thing is easy
I think
the government is also a
human being
it is not a
a super a super
power
it is not a
god
he is also a man
a man
like you and me
so we must pray for him
honestly we must prey
there is nothing now
nobody can do anything
its god
the almighty
who did
all creation
creation
ja its difficult
Oh Lord
instead of going
and bringing
better now
it is bad eh bad hm

.   .

what does one do what does one do
how
does one
start
Nomsa   .
to do
whatsisname
undo
the hard laws
the laws
you eh you

know
the government
knows
the authorities
know
they know
which laws
before
there was nothing
like this
before
.   .
when
in your time
Nomsa   .
yes
honestly
it was not like this aah
I don't think
it was like this
I never experienced this hardships
there were no passes at the
time
no
what happened
what went wrong now
wha where
did the the frightening come
huh
whereabout
we used to stay with people
in town in the district
what happened now
I am asking
that is a question
I am just surprised
I am asking my
brains
what went wrong
did the crime rate

rise
so that we are to be
away
from the where we were
we liked this people
we were
we worked for people
close
we like the people we work for
we like them
I think it was because of the
start
of the hard laws
the laws of fiar law fiar lawlawlaw
now these laws brought
something that we can be
frightened
of
there was no frightening before
at the time
I gre up
9491
I knew I had a brain at that time
I knew I can count from there
I didn't hear of any hardships
    .   .
but they must start
soon
or not
Nomsa   .
S
OOOOOOOOOOOOOOOOOOOOOO
                              n
^tog soon
this this
our Acirfa Huos
its wonderfully good
its beautiful
if people

can cooperate and then
the people
can work the
fields industry
and I don't know what
I am just saying
I don't know
I am also blind
but I see
this light
this light
that I have already mentioned
I think that is the
better thing

.   .

which
light
Nomsa   .
the light
that says
that the laws
must be
little bit
the laws
not even little bit
can be mended
not little bit
yes
as far as
the laws are concerned
they are
the small things
that
are wrong

.   .

which
Nomsa   .
Ha
you must not walk here
you see

the green manmust be
taught discipline
there are a lot of them that are
frightening
we know that
our people

.   .

what
I mean
how must it be done
the little laws must change
you mean
you can go
to any beach
Nomsa   .
if
the people
are
decent

.   .

if the people are
Nomsa   .
decent
if they
behave
ja
if they behave
ja
I don't say that people who come
and rule
the people
there now
on the beach
ja
they can be chased
away
ja everywhere
you can't stay
if you don't behave
haha

if you don't behave you can't stay anywhere
.   .
all the good
blue people
are
leaving
Nomsa   .
that is
also sad
all the good ones
that working
here
that worked
here
Zolile   .
I now want to say
something
because I
cry
I cry myself
according to my rent
to that I pay
i go this house
i stay this roof
is plain is nothing
nothing
I get in the house
but the rent
always going high
but my pay
ever down
with now they give
aaaaaaaaaa whaawhaaa whaaa whaa
with the pay young people
eeeevveevve even totoototototot
that there therer is
now
a sales tax
now
the rent

now now n
caanacaaan caaan
just like you see
you pay because you like
to stay here
now
we want to staaaaay
ok
its alright
Arthur   .
what i want to say
is we like pleasure
and we like
to enjoy ourselves
but weaint got time

.   .

why
Arthur   .
we really are
poor
because we are poor
what we need to enjoy ourselves
we need money
to support
the famillies and all
that jazz
actually
I don't like to work
but I do it
to support
my family
I should be a
scholar
by now
but I could not   make it

.   .

what pleasure what pleasure
do you like

Arthur   .
like sports
like soccer
idon't worry myself about
shebeens
when I was a
scholar
I was also doing sport
and bioscope
any kind of sport
actually
but now I work
l ain't got time
to to
practise but now there is no
time
I work for
money
to support our family
that is all
so we aint got time
to enjoy ourselves
as far as we
need
 .   .
when
do you
work
Arthur   .
I have to get up
at five
in the afternoon
and come back at three
in the morning
and I sleep
during the day
this friend of mine
has got his own problems
which

he can say
himself
I would like
to go
to the beaches
to the beaches
all day
I can say that
I   like
to enjoy
the summertime
yes
we have not got enough
money

.   .

But
you have to work
to earn
money
Arthur   .
yes
my friend
has been in the work
he likes work
but still he does
not get
work
you never get work

.   .

why
is it difficult
for you to
go
to the beach
Arthur   .
we have
not got transports
pointsea and bergmuiz
is far from
agnayn
we like our beach

even
but we have no transport
its far
there is no transport
to go there
ja
there are no
busses
my father
had
a small dairy business
but it has problems
like
when you have your own business
you like
to see
it go up
that is the main thing
to make you
work
but the small business could not support the
whole family
of us
that is all
we depend on it
the business
we depend on it
but I
can't make it
my small brothers I
have to send to school
so I
have to go to work
now
we close
the business

.   .

why
did you have
to close the
business

Arthur   .
there
was
no money to carry
on
.   .
why
did it
lose money
Arthur   .
support
.   .
people
did not buy
Arthur   .
they bought
they bought
it was not
well organised
.   .
the business
was not
well organised
Arthur   .
No No
it was very
poor
that is why I have closed it
that is why I am going to work
that is why I have to work
I just need money to
help
the business
but
there is no way
.   .
No
money
to get to start

the business
Arthur   .
that is why
I am working
only
that money to pick up
the business
my father
is old
my mother
is old
they give
the business
to me
but I could not make it
myself
.   .
how much
money
would you need to have
to pick up
the business
Arthur   .
I don't need more
than
S100
100 Sands
not more
it is
even difficult to
get that
S100
it is very difficult
to get the
S100
in the hands
even when I am working
it is still the same
you have got
to pay rent

support children to school
eat
all those
work
I get S40 a
month
I mean
S40 per week
Ja Ja
when I am doing
overtime
when I am not doing
overtime
I only get S30 per week
and
I have got three scholars
at home

.   .

your brothers
Arthur   .
it is
two brothersand one sister

.   .

how
old
are you
Arthur   .
I am
now o12
I have left school in 3191
when I left
Standard (
I didn't just leave
it
for pleasure
there was no money to

.   .

what
would you do
with the S100

Arthur   .
just
to put in
some stock
that is all
that I need
to sell
.   .

and
you can't
get the money from
a bank
Arthur   .
from a bank
.   .

they will not give you the money
Arthur   .
they don't
borrow
us money
even for the big
business man
here
it is very difficult
to get money
no no
the blues
they can go to the bank
and get a certain loan
and bring it back
but here
that thing
is very serious
you won't get it
unless
it is somebody
of your family
and that one you have to
speak many times
many times

so that he can
understand
your problem
not just give
people people
are very stingy
because because
they themselves are
struggling
they are struggling
themselves
but you won't get 20%
of us with money
you will only get
3
4
5
%
most of us are
very poor

.   .

and
what is rich
what is rich
to you
Arthur   .
I
I
I
get

.   .

what is rich
Arthur   .
rascals

.   .

what
Arthur   .
rascals

there are many of them
because
of this hunger
that is why
they are like this
they would like to
grab
people   for
money
and all that jazz
there is a lot of them
we grab each other
like mad people
because
they are starved

.   .

and
what is rich
what is rich
to you
to eat
Arthur   .
what is rich

.   .

you said
there are 5%
who are rich
Arthur   .
i mean
people
those people
those greens
there are only 5%
rich people
people who have got
money
got money money

.   .

and
what is that

how much is that
Arthur   .
that
percentage

.   .

No
how much money
do they have
Arthur   .
they have
got money
to
afford
their problems
their own problems
they are people
who have got
enough
to afford
their problems
whereas
most of us
well definately
each and everybody
needs
to have his own
life
for in summertime
now
to go to the beaches
for me
or we had that small business
and we did not even have a transport
to go to the
markets
to get
maybe
some greens or some fruit
to put
into the dairy
if
I had enough money

I should be far
by now
because the business was
flying then
there were a lot of people
buying there
it is flying
everything
but there is only one
one
the support at home
it is them
who is dragging
the business
down
the support
and can't do otherwise
there is nobody who
can be working
there
is only me
then my mother
sends
the small boy
to the business
need some sugar
need some coffee
and all that jazz
and I got to
give it
.   .
your
mother
Arthur   .
Ja
father
I need some cigarettes
ain't got money
he says
need some cigarettes

I got to take out money
and
give it to him
.   .
let us say
that you start
the business again
and your father comes
and he says
I need something
but I got no money
what
do you
do
Arthur   .
at least
by now
i have tried to support
the scholars
at least
as far as now
my smallest sister
is going to leave now
6.15
is going away to the homelands
with all their school things
because they open
now

.   .
but
what do you do
if your father
sais says
he needs something and
he has not got money
if you give
the stock away for
nothing
the business

will collapse
Arthur   .
it will collapse
as is
the first
No
what I think
as I mean
I will not just drop
the job
i am doing now
I will take the money
from there and
get some other stock
like sweets peanuts
these small things
for the children
vegtables
and they can do a stand
there
at home
at their own time
she will sell that and
support the family
Zolile   .
my problem is
this
why I I IIIIII
say
at first we
green people
here
in
acirfa
we we
pay the rent
the house of the councils
yes
now there is no floor

no roof
no nothing
you must pay
all
with your own money
but
you must pay the
rent
every month
they don't care now
we you we you you
we they do gone
to be after
to pay
ororoeoeoroahahahahaaaa
still you going to get
our
and you understand
that   is   why I   say   you
knoooooooow waawhat we We
to be
generous
to us
we can't
its
we can't
obey
we can't obey it
together together
.   .
can't understand
Zolile   .
together
the one with the money
the one he aint got the money
she must think about him
he she
because we work for
the state

because we are also people
of the state
that is to why
now
we together must get together
together we can all work
can be built the
spirit
because the spirit is
the people
the spirit
no spirit
they die
haaugh

.   .

why
do you drink so much
drink
so much
Zolile   .
yes
its its
why we drink to much
if of course
you must go to get the pay
as we work
because we work
like everybody
but the state
the state they give
aaah you know aahhaah
can say
aaahaahaah
they
green is eating on nothing
the yellow
eating higher
now they eat everything
now that is why

but we do the same work
we are doing
.   .
but
why the drink
Zolile   .
they are drinking because
why
they are oppressed
now
they don't think
they never go anywhere
yes
look
I say to you
you see
we never get the
house
you you must keep out money money
to make the house
your house
you never get the the house
like the
we like the same
everything Yaaa Yaaah
I am hungry
because
we don't get nothing on the state
you work for the state but
he state
don't give you nothing
.   .
but what
must they give you
don't they give you
Zolile   .
Ya
little little
and

they take it back
again
is is is
like new now
now we talk
I rent this house
.   .
how much does the rent
cost
Zolile   .
my rent cost
S8
per month
.   .
but that is
not much
Zolile   .
it is
much
much because
how much
I earn
yes
.   .
How much
do you earn
Zolile   .
S20
.   .
a month
Zolile   .
a week
look now
I must pay pay
we must eat
we must wear
we must school
and now

and so I say come
and
because we
the people of the state
we work for the state
and now
must come
we ashamed
ashamed
because he must look
after his people
the state
now
we must work for them
look
where we stand
look look
sir
and see
.   .
and
you
Pakamile   .
eeee
.   .
your name
talk
why you change
it
from english
Pakamile   .

eeeehahaha
hahahahahaha
hahahahahaha
Nomsa   .
look
an account from the
furniture people

pay pay pay
with the paying
but there is no written thing saying
you are now ending
the the whatisname
the account
installments every month
no end
we don't say we are
wonderful
we are good
but honestly
we must know
what is left
there
.   .
how much
was it
Nomsa   .
eh
you know
the bed   was not new when
I bought it from the former
people who bought it from the former
people
eh
but the store they send
every month the
pay pay pay
it says S355
how much
is that thing
eh
we are ignorant
about these things
we don't know
but we want to have
chairs to sit on
beds to sleep on
a house
when we have a house
so that is

why
we just fall in
eh
we have no time to
look
and we can not bring the chairs on our
hands
so eh
we have no cars
so we
just fall in
we are ignorant
eh
we get off little
only the mama
she gets off
eh
they don't like
women
and we want to go to our
homes
to the children
so when
can we
learn
eh

.   .
and you
Lungisa   .
what do you say
Lungisa   .
nothing

they spend
more than they
earn
on things like
drinks
hard drinks

57

.   .
why
Lungisa   .
they say that
they use
hard drinks to avoid
their worries and all that
.   .
but
what worries
Lungisa   .
eh that is what
I think
I always hear
those people who have
drink
it
our mistakes
they say that they
use hard drinks to avoid
worries and all that jazz
.   .
but then you'll
never get rid of the
worries
Lungisa   .
we will
never get rid
we will
always need some
money
because that is
waste waste
.   .
but how do you
stop
the people drinking
Lungisa   .
there is
no way
no way of stopping

them
somebody just leaves
drink
when he is satisfied
they do carry on
for a long time
after years
then
you see
someone leave the drink
someone go to the church
someone go to the sports
and all that jazz
when he is tired
himself
no one can tell him
to leave the drink
by by
telling him
they don't
in our society even the
scholars do the same
they smoke they drink
but
they are all in need of
money
for other things
not for pleasure smokes
smokes
those are things
just for pleasure
just to enjoy yourselves
•   •
but they do
they start
if they used their money
instead of for
drink they could build
up
Lungisa   •
they don't do it

you get the most poor people
the most poor people
are the most drinkers
the most you get
can

.   .

why
Lungisa   .
I don't know
why
some are those who are just
avoiding worries
eh they can't do
otherwise
they have no money
they are poor
they drink a lot
Zolile   .
you wake up
in the morning
there
now you buy
the Cape TomesExpress Rapport
we they
are talking
we know we know
what the   changes   they talk
that is why we go
on spirit
because drink
drink
tototototo drink
you keep your worries

.   .

to drink
you keep your worries
Zolile   .
Yeeesss

.   .

But
don't you want to

get rid of your worries
Zolile   .
because nobody can help you
nobody
can help
you
i f you cry
bah bah
you are crying
you cry
Pakamile   .
don't cry
you don't cry
somebody else of you
cries
me me
cries
because my brother
is shoot shoot
talk truth
what do you say
you shoot him
you have been shoot
dead
about your truth
you been talking
now
I cry because you be
shooted
now
I cry because my brother
dies because he
is talking the truth

.   .
what
is the
truth
Zolile   .
truth
aah
nobody
is got the truth

nobody because
people
ah peopple ah
in fact eh we
we are human beings
men with children like me
we must carry on
buthowwww
we
our children
must carry one and
they they they
grow
Arthur   .
each
and everybody
8 9 10
depends on the
inspectors
the pass
i had no record
by the offices
I have been doing
nothing wrong
I am
no criminal
I
pay pay
ah my taxes
my everything
my home
as well
I am paying all those jazz
I owe
the state nothing
but they do raid us
why don't you work and all that jazz
they keep us
in jail
for such rubbishes
those business

the passes
those reasons
I see
no need unless
you have had re
a bad record
you are a criminal
so maybe
they must know that if
I am not working
I am doing crime all around
and if they know
I am no criminal
maybe
I am trying
another better life
to lead
try
some of use don't want to work
and they do
small businesses
maybe you have a small place
you sell greens
do anything

.   .

why
don't they want to work
Arthur   .
because
some
I don't see
benefit for working
because you can work your
your your

.   .

your arms
Arthur   .
your arms
and gaining no money

for that
but if you set
small business
maybe you can even gain
a lot
of money like that
you can sell to the people
here
and gain a lot
but you usually get caught for
not working
which is unnessary
in some cases
but in some cases
that is neccessary
there are rascals
but maybe
nobody
is written
rascal
on his face
they won't know
who
they won't know
the people
who are around who always grab
the people
there are many crimes
unknown
eh you
the man who taked all the money
the Soudie
he had not rascal written all over his face
there are many crimes
maybe that is why
we are raided like
flies
every morning

Zolile   .
we can get
nowhere eh
we are also
acirfans
eh now
we are working
why why

.   .

why what
why what
Zolile   .
wIIIIIIIIIII
look
the state
must look
after his people
combine

.   .

combine
Zolile   .
yes
combine
with the
with the
blue people
Pakamile   .
you get a green and blue flower
Arthur   .
some of
our fathers
they are old
and they have worked their
strength out
but they still have
not got the money
they have been working for
blue people
but they are old
now

.   .

why
don't you kill

the blue people
then
why don't you kill them
Arthur   .
why

  .   .

why
Arthur   .
why what
you can do is just to
talk
instead of
killing
because we don't need
to be killed ourselves
so then
there is no need
that there is somebody
who has got to be killed
what we can do is
talk together
and
live together
and
be   together
thats all

  .   .

Lungisa
Lungisa   .
Well
I have got nothing
to say
at the moment
I do
see
some things
which are unfavourable
somehow

  .   .

which
are what

Lungisa   .
so much
to see

.   .

speak
speak from the heart
Lungisa   .
ah
ah
we would
like
to have
our own
houses
but you can't get that
our own
roads
tarred
but
in some other places
some other places
like
the vaalavant
they are given
their homes
ah
they
own their homes
and
eh
they buy their homes
ah

.   .

what else
Lungisa   .
ehhaah

.   .

what else what else
Lungisa   .
ah eh ahah
I would like

to see
the reference books
they give us
a lot of trouble
somehow

.   .

how
Lungisa   .
we must
go
to the Green Administration
Board
for their signature
every time
eh
every time
the duration
they
give you
expires
you must go
there

.   .

every time
you do
what
Lungisa   .
every time
they
every   time
the duration expires

.   .

how long
are
they
Lungisa   .
if you are
a worker
a labourer
you are given
10 days

to look for a job
if
you don't get a job
in that time
you must go
and tell
them
that you
did not get a job
so they must extend
must give
you an extention
·   ·
every
10 days
Lungisa   ·
ja
·   ·
until you get a job
and as a
normal person
if
you live here
how often
must Nomsa go
to get it extended
Nomsa   ·
seven
days
sometimes
seven days
if you don't get work
seven days
but now
I don't worry
too much
I don't get that
because
i am a
wifehouse
but others

69

the unmarried
they are given
seven days
to look for a job

.   .

and
if they don't
find a job
what happens
Nomsa   .
then
you pass is
thrown into the dustbin

.   .

and then
Nomsa   .
you don't
have a pass
then
you go and drinking
and then
you don't get a job
and then
you are always arrested
because of pass
because you did not get job
that seven days
Lungisa   .
after that
you are sent
to the country
without money
without nothing
Nomsa   .
that is
the thing
the hard
thing

.   .

Lungisa
does not want

to talk
Nomsa   .
he
never likes to talk
he
is a quiet person
he
say he does not like
politics
I say
politics are the
thing
politics
I say
the only thing
we know
is
apartfiar
we don't know
any other thing
you see
its funny
but then its true
as I say
the politics is apartfiar
that is the
word
we don't know
any other
thing
as I told you
if
we can be given
amenities
facilities
yes
that are enjoyed by
other nations
in Acirfa
because there are
people of us who are

dignified
we can behave like
the other nations
I know there are many of
our people who are as you
say
rascals
and nobody can mix with people
who are
misbehaving like
this
you also become
disappointed
the weather
outside
is bad
towards people
towards people
the inner side of the people
the inner hearts are disappointed
you see
that is why
people like to destroy themselves
now that
is why Zolile
drinks
the inside is disappointed
he is
dead
it
because of those laws
yes
he was frightened
to tell you
why daydreaming
daydreaming
it is because   they have got
to much hardships
the lot
of hardships

there now
they want to quench
to quench
all these troubles
by drinking
they think
it is the right way

.   .

so
they try and
destroy the inside
Nomsa   .
to destroy
the brain
or anything that is
thinking
the part of the brain
of the head
he does not know
he is making it worse
he lose his job
he lose his job
there is no place
where
you can stay
drunk
nobody wants you
but they have chosen
the alternative
between
good and bad

.   .

what alternative
Nomsa   .
the bad one
as is
good and bad
to destroy and to build
they have chosen the
alternative

I don't know
if I am right with the tive
alternative
they have chosen the badness
the destroying
side
can't pay the rent
and they have got
nowhere to sit
to stay
if they can't work
that's the
thing
that
all the words
are trying to go to
this one thing
they have got to know
they they
have got no one to
prepare the hardships
to make it good
the
hard soft
a little bit
to make the opposite of
hardness hardships
.   .
and
how do they do that
just by
relaxing the pass
laws
Nomsa   .
yes
and by   by   leaving it
all all all
up to
eh eh
Zolile   .
eheh II

look
at the eyes
the eyes
are so
eh eyegene
ey
.   .
I
wanted to ask
ask you
why do you
now Lungisa says
if he wants to make a
phone call
he must walk to
a kneighbour
who has one
and must pay
60 grains
why do some of the
green people
take so much
from the other ones who
don't have anything
Nomsa   .
because
they must pay for
their
private telephones
.   .
but
a call cost
10 grains
but the phone call
costs
only 10 grains
Nomsa   .
which

.   .
the one lungisa
says
be must make
if it costs
10 grains
why must they charge
60 grains
Nomsa   .
because
they pay
a lot

.   .
but
it only costs
10 grains
Nomsa   .
they say
they pay
a lot
for installing
for putting it
.   .
sometimes
the blue man
says
if you help a green
and
lets say
be does not drink it
he uses it
but then
in english
in english
says
be rips off
the
Nomsa   .
eh eh

rips off

.   .

uh
Nomsa   .
he can't
help it
he is
so poor

.   .

he ripps
off
the other greens
Nomsa   .
he is poor
he is poor
he is
the only one
who has got
the

.   .

but but
Lungisa   .
because
that
is
the
only way
he
can
survive
Nomsa   .
that is it
that's it

.   .

by taking
taking
Nomsa   .
yes
yeas

.   .

by taking from
the green
that is the only way he can survive
Nomsa   .
yees
eh
we don't worry
because
we don't
help it
we think
he is so
so high
we go to him
we say
please
we need
kneel down
Lungisa   .
that is
the way
it is

.   .

they say
what costs in
bluemont
a bottle of beer or
I don't know
something
say 40 grains
costs
here
in the townships
80 grains why
Liziwe   .
the busfares
is beating us
you know from
here
to bluemont

it is 50 grains
and then I
am going to buy the
sane thing
there
it is cheaper
to buy it
here
at 80 grains
.   .
but
buy in bulk
Liziwe   .
eh
and how
do we
carry it
on
the bus
alone
and the
tsotsis
kill us
anywhere we have
no fridges so
we can't keep it
the trouble
is also this
they don't allow us
all the drinks
we have to go and buy
from them
once they find
that you
are selling the
beers and some other things
they want
liscences
but they won't

let us have a
liscence
for the beer
or for the drinks
they don't allow
it
where ever we are trying
to make something
they
h ave got not to let
them
know that we are
selling something
.   .
otherwise
they stop you
Liziwe   .
they
don't stop
they
just take you
straight to jail
and
you have got   to go
and pay
and pay
yourself
ah ah fine
of   about
50 Sands
or
75 sands
or
100 Sands
for selling
without a liscence
although it is not
you know I can
understand them
if they just want to
stop us   to sell
something like

dagga
or the eh eh
you see
but we are selling
these cheap stufflike
cooldrinks and everything
they want us to pay
liscence
for those things
it is about seventy five sands
if they find you
selling those things
that is why we are
so poor
like this
and that
is why there are lots of
tsotsis
because our children
are getting
its too much
hunger
at our place
you see
no else you see
we are
the mothers
and
the fathers
we can't make
business
to feed our children
you see
sometimes a son of this age
has
still got to go to school
but the mother
can't afford
to pay

the school fees
and everything for this
son
and then this
son
just
leave leave leave
the school
you see
and then that is
why
the tsotsis
are starting this business
because
he is always hungry
he wants to
get something to eat
and I
can't afford to buy
a loaf of bread
for him
because
I am also
single
you see
weather I have got a pass
if I can't get a
job
they will just take off
my pass
from me
and then
they
will say
they
are going to send me to
keiavant
and i
was never
never
born

i n
the keiavant
I I
this
is where I was born
I don't know
how
can I live
in the keiavant
that
is the trouble with
us
sometimes
your children
you have got about five children
they can't have
food
for about three days
that
it why
some of   them
u
just walk around
and then they can get
a piece
of
old
stale
bread
from the street
and then they
just pick it up
and eat
those who have got no
ands
that is why the
old ones
they just grab

things
money
from people
like that
and then
they kill people and
they don't mean to do it
but
it is
from their hunger
they they
and you can
seee
here
if you walk about
from the cats up to
the dogs up to
people
dog is the second thing
they all lookuohook
so funny
because they
can't afford
to pay
we want to have all these things
and we are willing
to do
the jobs
you know what
they
are doing
here
in goodhope
they
are especially taking the
men from the keiavant
to do the jobs
here
first
habannina is a saying
all the time

that he
has got jobs
for his people
we
are not
    his people
we
were born here in
goodhope
but we can't afford
to look after our own
our families
because
there is   not
money for us
and we
are
willing to work
but
no
jobs
that is the trouble
with us
you see
I don't blame these children
who
just grab
money from people
you see
they can't do
otherwise
they are so
hungry
here
they have not even
got
something to
wear

.   .

how
do you

start with finding a
job
Nomsa   .
Liziwe   .
Pardon

.   .

you told me
me
without a liscence
you can't start
any business
here
Liziwe   .
I can
if
you can
try and get a liscence
for me
you must apply for the
liscence
because
if they find me selling
peaches oranges and everything
then
they are
just going to take me
to jail
and then
I am going to pay
seventy five sands

.   .

where
do you
get the liscence
Liziwe   .
I
apply for it
its not to difficult
to apply
but
sometimes we don't know

how
to apply
and we must
wait eh
eh
you know the
big trouble
with us is this
if you have not got some
eh
little money to
start
it is
vvveeerrryyy
seldom you get a
business

.   .

how much
is
little money
Liziwe   .
I think
if you can get
about
a
hundred and fifty sands
that
would be really a
good start
and then
we can say that
eh
that he failed

.   .

failed what
Liziwe   .
if he failed
to prove
a
business

but not with me
I promise
its a lot of money
but the trouble with
a dairy is
the electric
you have to keep
the the
those whatsis name
and and
everything
in the freezers
freezers
and ice creem for
the freezers
Arthur   .
I have
three children
at school
.   .
you
Arthur   .
yes
there is my
little brothers and sisters
I must help them
eh
and last
the last
year
they took our
higi hifi
because
we could not pay
I think we had paid
more
than half
only one third
is left
but they have

taken it
for ever
and what about
that money
we never get

if we need
another
we have got to pay
all again
eh
and I told that
them
that we are not going
to pay
we are going to pay
it
we are still trying
something
but they
they would not listen
to us
they
just take it away
Liziwe   .
we
are going
to help
you
.   .
what
I
don't understand
Nomsa   .
we
are with
you
we
are with
you

with prayers
and then
no body
and then
nothing can happen
to you
don't worry
Zolile   .
my home is
your home
it is
disappointing
the people
are
so greedy
eh
Nomsa   .
ndilapa nkosi
ndilapa e
nkosi
iwas
i was
a sinner
but then
the great one helped me
but goodness
is
not wanted here
but we
believe in
it
we believe in
the goodness of
ourselves
that we are
good
that our lives
are
worth living

we try and bring
ourselves
up
they don't like it
but we wait
until
the time
we are
here
waiting
the sign will come
in a
funny way
when we
least
are waiting
in trying to get a house
and in being a mother
in looking after the children
this was not done by the government
we look
for the spirit
we look
to find the spirit
of god inside us
he will give something
inside us
we must concentrate and
think of that
which is happening
to look and see
then there is something
there is something inside you
and you will not more be able
to fiar
people apart
you will understand
you will have a feeling
for people
they are human beings

the lord made you
the feelings are
inside
you no longer want
bad people
it is not that you don't
want them
they are also people
but you don't want to
mix
with them
the people are crying
they are crying
we must look around
and see
what is wrong with
you
this thing we must look around
and see
where it is wrong
and the people in power must look around
look and look
and see and see
why
the people are crying
he
the person who has got the power
must try and fix
these things
ah
that we all have a
little
power.

Glossary/Dramatis Personae

Ndi	I	
lapa		Am here, here.
Nkosi		Lord
Ndilapa Nkosi		I am here Lord/Here I am Lord
Arthur	.	Arthur
Liziwe	.	Giving Child
Lungisa	.	Goodness
Nomsa	.	Sympathy, affectionate
Pakamile	.	High one
Zolile	.	Quietness
.	.	Inner voice/nameless character

Etienne Leroux and Samuel Beckett

E/OmOtLevinson
" Omutara " ,
St James Road
St James 7945
Cape Town
Rep. of South Africa
12th June 1979

Mr Samuel Beckett
c/o Faber and Faber ,
3 Queens Square
London WC 1
United Kingdom .

Dear Mr Beckett ,

I need your help .

Either I am practising gross self-deception or else your acknowlegement of my existence is needed .

I feel that the enclosed play Ndilapa Nkosi owes much to you but does not resemble . We are differentgenerations and have diffesent experiences and outlooks on man and the world .

It has been said that the play breaks new ground ; and that I should send it toyou with an accompanying interpretation . I can't do this . I can only say that if you see merit it would be better all round for me to make my way to see you personally . Also I can say that for me the play has significance - all I want to say now is that the Names could be made up but at the deeper level do have significance . Ndilapa Nkosi is Xhosa for I am here Lord . Ndilapa e nkosi is Xhosa for I am here thankyou ; Nomsa- sympayhy , Lungisa -goodness , Zolile quietness Pakamile thigh one Liziwe -giving child . FOr me the relationship is not black and white , but any primary secondary relationship . I talk too much .

May I burden you with one favour . If nothing could you return the play to me registerred post at the above address . I could only find 20 French francs to cover this .

P.O. Box 60,

KOFFIEFONTEIN.

O.F.S.

Dear Orde,

I am fascinated by you lyrical comedy. I like th
refrains & incantations based on Xhosa, Afrikaans-cum-
English etc. The way you use ironic interpolations
in an African style of speech. There is a rhythm that is
most catching and an underlayer of haunting sadness.
It is indeed a satiric statement of mans estate : Ndilapa
Nkosi. I like the use of the blue people and the green
people because the blue and the green are nn different
combinations
/ixxxix of the complimentary colours. (Red-green; blue-
yellow). That was a clever and very ironic find.

But you see

eh eh

I am a greenhorn.

I love your lyrical comedy, but who am I to say ?
This is an experience in another medium than my own. I
think Athol Fugard would be the better judge.

But I like it. Ekamile. There is a beginning, but
no end. Already your lyrical comedy is haunting me, shah !

Yours ever,
Etienne Leroux.

95

Paris
21.7.79

SAMUEL BECKETT

Dear ? O'Dell

I am not qualified
to comment on this work,
beyond that it is a moving
text.

I do not understand why
you call it a play.

With apologies for my
incompetence & all good
wishes, yrs. sincerely
Samuel Beckett

P.O. Box 60,

KOFFILFONTEIN.

Dear Orde,

Yes, I would like a copy of Ndilapa Nkosi for myself. As a present from you. Have you read any of my books ? If not/~~IXIX~~ I'll pick the book that I will send/to you in return. ~~ixxzzxkxnxxxfxx~~ A quid pro qou. Yes, I can use Ndilapa. Quidni ? I was always bad at Latin. I am stupid. I am the/~~stupixixx~~ stupisded writer abroad. Words do not mean a thing to max grammatically I like the sound of words; the meaning beyond grammar; the ultimate connection of the third kind. I think I am a bad influence, Orde. Perhaps not. I am not sure.

I am amazed at the guts that you had to send a copy of your book to Beckett. I would have been too scared. Just the fact that he found it "moving" is praise beyond comprehension. Famous writers like Beckett do not write a "card" in reply. They usually ignore the thousand supplications. Is the Old Man still alive ? He must be a Vampyre, 600 A.C.

Please continue writing, Orde. Your first letter was not "nasty". Don't destroy your works. Try Athol Fugard.

Yd you. 9 My Lavan Press

er, Etienie Leroux

Transcripts

P.O. Box 60,

KOFFIEFONTEIN

O.F.S.

Dear Orde,

I am fascinated by you lyrical comedy. I like the refrains & incantations based on Xhosa, Afrikaans-cum-English etc. The way you use ironic interpolations in an African style of speech. There is a rhythm that is most catching and an underlayer of haunting sadness. It is indeed a satiric statement of mans's estate : Ndilapa Nkosi. I like the use of the blue people and the green people because the blue and the green are different combinations of the complimentary colours. (Red-green; blue- yellow). That was a clever and very ironic find.

But you see

eh eh

I am a greenhorn.

I love your lyrical comedy, but who am I to say? This is an experience in another medium than my own. I think Athol Fugard would be the better judge.

But I like it. Pakamile. There is a beginning, but no end. Already our lyrical comedy is haunting me, ahah!

Yours ever,

Etienne Leroux

Paris

21.7.79

SAMUEL BECKETT

I am not qualified to comment on this work, beyond that it is a moving feat.

I do not understand why you call it a play.

With apologies for my incompetence & all best wishes.

Yours Sincerely

Samuel Beckett

P.O. Box 60,

KOFFIEFONTEIN.

Dear Orde,

Yes, I would like a copy of Ndilapa Nkosi for myself. As a present from you. Have you read any of my books ? If not I'll pick the book that I will send to you in return. A quid pro qou. Yes, I can use Ndilapa. Quidni ? I was always bad at Latin. I am stupid. I am the stupisded writer abroad. Words do not mean a thing to me grammatically. I like the sound of words; the meaning beyond grammar; the ultimate connection of the third kind. I think I am a bad influence, Orde. Perhaps not. I am not sure.

I am amazed at the guts that you had to send a copy of your book to Beckett. I would have been too scared. Just the fact that he found it "moving" is praise beyond comprehension. Famous writers like Beckett do not write a "card" in reply. They usually ignore the thousand supplications. Is the Old Man still alive? He must be a Vampyre, 600 A.C.

Please continue working, Orde. Your first letter was not "nasty". Don't, destroy your works. Try Athol Fugard.

Yours and try Raven Press.

Ever,

Etienne Leroux

Reviews

BOOK REVIEW

Brave attempt by an 'outsider'

By Z B MOLEFE

THE FIRST reading of this exciting work offers a number of deceptions. But after it had been digested, a clearer picture emerges. This is a brave attempt towards South Africa's own "native" writing in the English language.

And, it will be easy for many to accuse the writer of this lyrical comedy — the first work of a trilogy — as one of those whites who write about us without knowing the "black man's situation in South Africa". Another deception, this reviewer will argue.

Goethe said: "The poet as a man and citizen will love his native land, but the native land of his poetic powers and poetic action is the good, noble and beautiful which is confined to no particular province or country and which he siezes upon and forms wherever he finds.

The writer of this work then adds with caution to that universally-accepted statement: "My work is of personal significance . . . My philosophy: conceptual realism. I don't wish to commit to paper any explanations regarding Ndilapha Nkosi. The work must tell its own tale. I can only hope that the work will move.

"I am not qualified to comment on this work, beyond that it is a moving feast," said Nobel Prize winner and master playwright Samuel Beckett, the publishers tell us.

The haunting beauty of the rolling hills of Natal's Valley of a Thousand Hills and the unspoilt beauty of places like Swaziland's Ezulwini Valley suddenly leap out of the pages when this poet gets going.

But it is the language that holds "Ndilapha Nkosi" and the ten other miscellaneous poems that make this collection. The refrains and incantations based on Xhosa, Afrikaans-cum-English become a definite pointer that the poet is striving for a South African "native" literature.

Social scientists, social workers, the police, the church and countless organisations have come up with a thousand-and-one reasons why black South Africans are victims of the "demon drink".

Runs the pen of the poet: "You also become disappointed/the weather outside is bad/towards people/towards people/the inner side of the people/the inner hearts are disappointed/you see that is why/people like to destroy themselves/now that is why Zolile drinks/the inside is disappointed/he is dead".

He rubs it in: "So they try and destroy the inside/Notna/to destroy the brain or anything that is thinking/the part of the brain/of the head/he does not know/he is making it worse/he loses his job/he loses his job/these is no place/where you can stay drunk/nobody wants you/but they have chosen/the alternative/between good

and bad/ On the other hand, that gifted South African writer Etienne Leroux, comes to the heart of the matter: "The way you (that is the poet Orde) use ironic interpolations is an African style of speech. There is a rhythm that is most catching and an underlayer of haunting sadness. It is indeed a satiric statement of man's estate: Ndilapha Nkosi."

And that statement of man's estate is expressed in that haunting language. In fact, this reviewer will be bold to say, this is a statement to the future of our beloved homeland, South Africa — "and the people in power must look around/look and look/and see and see/why the people are crying/he the person who has got the power/must try and fix/these things/ah that we all have/a little power . . ."

Remember in the introductory notes the poet warned that "I can only hope that the work will move." Well get yourself a copy and see if it does not move-Eh neh?

NDILAPHA NKOSI . . . by Orde Levinson (Ororey Publications, Cape Town — Price R4.95c)

'. . . It is the language that holds 'Ndilapha Nkosi' and the 10 other miscellaneous poems that makes this collection. The refrains and incantations based on Xhosa, Afrikaans-cum-English become a definite pointer that the poet is striving for a South African 'native' literature.'

101

Orde Levinson, *Ndilapa Nkosi*. Cape Town: Ororey Publications, 1981.
100 pp. Paperback.   R4,95

Enjoyment. Magic. Style. These were the trinity of a great teacher, Vladimir Nabokov, of Cornell University. He used every year to tell his class that literature is of no practical value whatsoever, except in the very special case of somebody's wishing to become, of all things, a professor of literature. Needless to say, he was his own living rebuttal of this tenet, holding fast — as he did — to his trinity.

So, too, with Orde Levinson: magic and style abound in this lyrical comedy (the first work of a trilogy), and the reader's enjoyment increases proportionately as the poem unfolds. This is 'outer and inner' poetry at its best: it is a statement of things as they are. Orde (for this is what the poet calls himself) makes poetry out of what the real subject of poetry should be: people. He is in effect charting the geometry of human existence here — South Africa — and in the universe. In this he is supported by his technique. There are no strained polysyllables, and there is thus no awkwardness in reading the poem aloud. The poem — and bear in mind that it is a very long poem — is strong and patterned, both compassionate and emphatic. It is clear, furthermore, that the poet has regarded any unrelated issue as deadwood, a twig of digression. The result is a poem that is neither turgid nor turbid, but a moving (and flowing) poetic statement:

Say
Something
Nomsa
Eh   (p.1)

and

... the
permit
pass
laws
how does it affect the family
Nomsa   (p.9)

and

It is
easy
the thing is easy
I think
the government is also a
human being   (p.25)

and so much more. Read this poem. After you have you will, I think, be able to say, along with other Southern African readers, 'Ndilapa Nkosi' — 'I am here, Lord'. Orde's poem is artwork. It is superb.

A.D. ADEY
Department of English
University of South Africa

Reviews' Transcripts

SOWETAN, Monday, May 25, 1981   Page 7

BOOK REVIEW

Brave attempt by an 'outsider'

THE FIRST reading of this exciting work offers a number of deceptions. But after it had been digested, a clearer picture emerges. This is a brave attempt towards South Africa's own "native" writing in the English language.

And, it will be easy for many to accuse the writer of this lyrical comedy - the first work of a trilogy - as one of those whites who write about us without knowing the "black man's situation in South Africa". Another deception, this reviewer will argue.

By Z B MOLEFE

Goethe said: "The poet as a man and citizen will love his   native Iand; but the native land of his poetic powers and poetic action is the good, noble and beautiful which is confined to no particular province or country and which he siezes upon and forms wherever he finds.

The writer of this work then adds with caution to that universally-accepted statement: "My work is of personal significance ... My philosophy; conceptual realism. I don't wish to commit to paper any explanations regarding Ndilapha Nkosi. The work must tell its own tale. I can only hope that the work will move.

"I am not qualified to comment on this work, beyond that it is a moving feat," said Nobel Prize winner and master playwright Samuel Beckett, the publishers tell us.

The haunting beauty of the rolling hills of Natal's Valley of a Thousand Hills and the unspoilt beauty of places like Swaziland's Ezulwini Valley; suddenly leap out of the pages when this poet gets going.

But it is the language that holds "Ndilapha Nkosi" and the ten other miscellaneous poems that make this collection. The refrains and incantations based on Xhosa, Afrikaans0cum-English become a definite pointer that the poet is striving for a South African "native" literature.

Social scientists, social workers, the police, the church and countless organisations have come up with a thousand-and-one reasons why black South Africans are victims of the "demon drink".

Runs the pen of the poet: "You also become disappointed/the weather outside is bad/towards people/towards people/the inner side of the people/the inner hearts are disappointed/you see that is why/people like to destroy themselves/now that is why Zolile drinks/the inside is disappointed/he is dead.

He rubs it in: "So they try and destroy the inside/Nomsa/to destroy the brain or anything that is thinking/the part of the brain/the head/he does not know/he is making it worse/he loses his job/he loses his job/there is no place/where you can stay drunk/nobody wants you/but they have chosen/the alternative/between good and bad/. On the other hand, that gifted South African writer Etienne Leroux, comes to the heart of the matter: "The way you (that is the poet Orde) use ironic interpolations is an African style of speech. There is a rhythm that is most catching and an underlayer of haunting sadness. It is indeed a satiric statement of man's estate: Ndilapha Nkosi"

And that statement of man's estate is expressed in that haunting language. In fact, this reviewer will be bold to say, this is a statement to the future of our beloved homeland, South Africa - "and-the people in power must look around/look and look/and see and see/why the people are crying/he the person who has got the power/must try and fix/these things/ah that we all have/a little power .."

Remember in the introductory notes the poet warned that "I can only hope that the work will move." Well get yourself a copy and see if it does not move. Eh neh?

NDILAPA NKOSI by Orde Levinson (Ororey Publications, Cape Town – Price R4,95c)

'... it is the language that holds 'Ndilapha Nkosi' and the 10 other miscellaneous poems that makes this collection. The refrains and incantations based on Xhosa, Afrikaans-cum-English become a definite pointer that the poet is striving for a South African 'native' literature.'

Orde Levinson, Ndilapa Nkosi. Cape Town: Ororey Publications, 1981.

100 pp. Paperback. R4.95

Enjoyment. Magic. Style. These were the trinity of a great teacher, Vladimir Nabokov, of Cornell University. He used every year to tell his class that literature is of no practical value whatsoever, except in the very special case of somebody's wishing to become, of all things, a professor of literature. Needless to say, he was his own living rebuttal of this tenet, holding fast — as he did — to his trinity.

So, too, with Orde Levinson: magic and style abound in this lyrical comedy (the first work of a trilogy), and the reader's enjoyment increases proportionately as the poem unfolds. This is 'outer and inner' poetry at its best: it is a statement of things as they are. Orde (for this is what the poet calls himself) makes poetry out of what the real subject of poetry should be: people. He is in effect charting the geometry of human existence here — South Africa — and in the universe. In this he is supported by his technique. There are no strained polysyllables, and there is thus no awkwardness in reading the poem aloud. The poem — and bear in mind that it is a very long poem — is strong and patterned, both compassionate and emphatic. It is clear, furthermore, that the poet has regarded any unrelated Issue as deadwood, a twig of digression. The result is a poem that is neither turgid nor turbid, but a moving (and flowing) poetic statement:

Say

Something

Nomsa

Eh   (p.1)

and

... the

permit

pass

laws

how does It affect the family

Nomsa   (p.9)

and

it is

easy

the thing is easy

I think

the government is also a

human being   (p.25)

and so much more. Read this poem. After you have you will, l think, be able to say, along with other Southern African readers, 'Ndilapa Nkosl' — 'I am here, Lord'. Orde's poem is artwork. It is superb.

A.D. ADEY

Department of English

University of South Africa

JANUARY 1982 .CRUX

Afterword: Printing; eBook; POD, Typeface.

Ndilapa Nkosi has a particular format where the placing of words, letters and its structure (including the double dot and in particular the 2nd dot) is an integral part of the work. It was written using a typewriter where the stroke gives a certain weight, width and depth not found with computer typefaces today. For example on page 20 of the work, where Nomsa says JJJAAA the typewriter has a width of each J equivalent to that of the A, or on page 66 of the work the word facilities typewriter written is longer than amenities, yet in computer typeface the automatic space adjustments reverse this – and trying to solve this problem by putting in extra spaces is not the same. On many occasions the original edition's spacing of Ndilapa Nkosi simply cannot be maintained where letters are placed clearly at set junctions in relation to letters above and below them on the same page, unless it is a facsimile reproduction.

For the eBook version the issue of a static v dynamic book arose as a difficult question with competing demands. Keeping this structure for eBook publication is only possible if it is transferred as static text but then, it is, I am told, self-defeating in terms of the benefits of eBooks, with its allowing of change of fonts, size, and its adaption to varying screen sizes or the ability to search for words. Furthermore the 2nd dot cannot have spaces between it but appears in a much shortened space, whereas it should have an indentation space as per the print on demand version, which is a close replica of the original typewritten publication. It needs to follow the other 2nd dot of the other voices. Another example not been able to be achieved with an eBook is on page 6 of the text (I have kept the original page numbers) the words 'live anywhere' is deliberately spaced away from the margin to allow the 'l' to fall below the 'h' of 'the blue'; and 2nd 'e' of 'anywhere' to end below the 'g' of 'green', making a link between the blue and green.

An eBook is a different dimension/medium for me and while I appreciate the raison d'etre of it, for example of allowing a reader to change texts and fonts, of searches in the text, which allows me to look at my work anew I instinctively feel this is too much latitude and too far from the original force and love that created the work especially where format is an integral part of the work – and the meaning shifts, which while it might be interesting, is in a sense illegitimate. However I need to give this format a chance with a work like Ndilapa Nkosi, and see what it brings forth – in a sense to be dynamic not static. I look forward and would welcome any thoughts and feedback on this issue. For this printed edition the production designer has done the best possible – and it is a close copy of the authentic version with all its wonderful typewriter typed visual nuances and meanings, that original edition of six, two of which were sent to Beckett and Le Roux. It is not exact as on page 7 the typed version could have in line 10 the "I" exactly below and above the "y" of you and "t" of not; or on page 9 where with a typewriter his and her are equal in length but with a computer the her is longer.

orde Oxford, 9 April 2014

Dedication

To Etienne,
To Samuel.
Et tu, Brute?
you were the first –
are -:

the lot.
Orde

July 1979

Note by the Author 1980

Regarding myself: I am not a politician and my work has no such overtones. Picasso, once asked what his political affiliations were, replied: 'In Spain there is a king, therefore I am a royalist.'

My work is of personal significance be it an expression of a manifold world or be it of moral or historical significance. Goethe said: 'The poet as a man and citizen will love his native land; but the native land of his poetic powers and poetic action is the good, noble and beautiful which is confined to no particular province or country and which he seizes upon and forms wherever he finds.' As such, my maxim: 'tel homme, tel artiste, tel vie.' My philosophy : conceptual realism.

I don't wish to commit to paper any explanations regarding Ndilapa Nkosi.

The work must tell its own tale.

I can only hope that the work will move.

Orde

September 1980

Note by the Publisher 2013

Mæg ic be me sylfum   I can make a true song

soðgied wrecan,   about me myself,

The Seafarer, date unknown. (Approximate translation of the old English)

Song, established in 2013 is an imprint of a new publication house, a division of Song of the Wild Swan Ltd.

It publishes any writings from anyone who has a song.

Song also participates in the BEL (Barter Exchange Levy) Price System.

List of Selected Works by orde

Song, November 2013
Areas of classification may overlap

Books

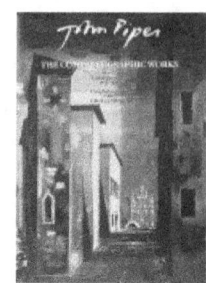

1   *John Piper – The Complete Graphic Works: A
     Catalogue Raisonné 1923-1983.* Compiled and
     edited by Orde Levinson. Faber & Faber,
     1988.

2   *I Was Lonelyness: The Complete Graphic Works
     of John Muafangejo 1968-1987.* Struik
     Winchester, 1992. Foreword by Archbishop
     Desmond Tutu. Contributing essays from:
     Olga Levinson (The Life and Art of John
     Muafangejo); Edward Lucie-Smith (John
     Muafangejo); Pat Gilmour (On Not Being a
     Political Artist); Orde Levinson (John
     Muafangejo, Cubism and Traditional African

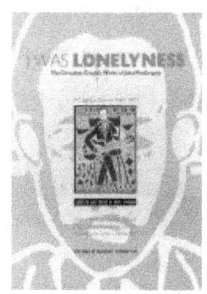

     Art); Olga Levinson (The Historical
     Development of Art in Namibia) and Steven
     Sack (The Rorke's Drift Art and Craft
     Centre) and all Muafangejo's Interviews,
     Statements and published conversations.

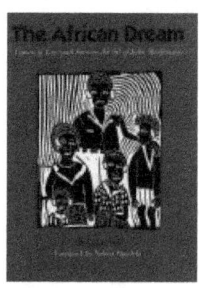

3   *The African Dream – Visions of Love and
     Sorrow. The Art Of John Muafangejo.* Thames
     and Hudson, 1993. Foreword by Nelson
     Mandela.

4   *Quality and Experiment. The Prints of John
     Piper – A Catalogue Raisonné.* Lund
     Humphries, 1996.

5   *The Prints of John Piper – A Catalogue Raisonné
     1921-1991.* Lund Humphries, 2010.
     Contributing essays: Introduction (Orde
     Levinson); Experiment and Quality (Orde
     Levinson); Subject and Technique in Piper's
     Printmaking (David Fraser Jenkins); Working
     with Printers (John Piper).

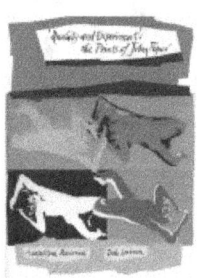

6   *Hitting the Nail on the Head – The Complete Written Works of John Piper 1913-1992.* An estimated three volumes with contributing essays by various authors (tba). Scheduled for publication 2014/5.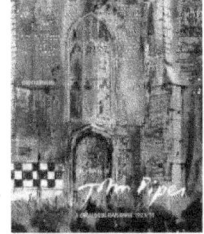

7   *Delights and Aphorisms, selected writings of John Piper.* Scheduled for publication 2014-5.

8   *Daniel Henry Kahnweiler: A bibliography.* Scheduled for publication 2014.

9   *The Life and Work of Daniel Henry Kahnweiler: A critical evaluation.* Originally part of the D. Phil. Study at Magdalen College, Oxford University. Scheduled for publication 2015.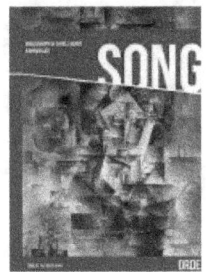

10 *The Complete Writings of Daniel Henry Kahnweiler.* Three volumes. Scheduled for publication 2015-6.

Conversations and interviews

11 *orde's Conversations with Henry Moore.* Henry Moore talks about influences, the artists he likes, his work and life in general. Available as eBook 2013 Book published by Song 2014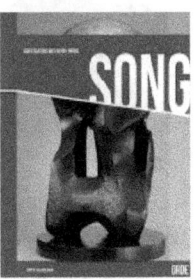

12 *Orde's Conversations with Richard Sorabji (videoed)* in progress,. Richard Sorabji in thought and in person is brought to us in a unique experiment where orde has selected friends from each decade to converse with him. Completed to date are Louis Hynes (age 10); Laurence Hutton-Smith (age 20); Richard Kuziara (age 37); Lisa Hammond-Marty (age 40-50); Jeremy Rowe (age 50-58); Marianne Talbot (age 58--68) Joanna Foster (age 68-80). Available as video, eBook and book. Scheduled publication 2015.

13 *Talking to Solly Irwin (videoed)* Schedule publication as eBook and book 2014-5,

Films

14   *Essences*. Independent production produced by orde under the inspiration of Straub and Huillet. A contemplative mood piece starring Richard E. Grant and Kiki Savejan
Director/script/editor: orde
Cast: Richard E Grant, Kiki Savejan
Running Time: 40 minutes/colour
Date Completed: 1983
(Image: Scene Shot from Essences by orde.)

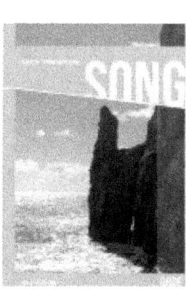

15   *Ÿ*
Director/script/editor: orde
Cast: Richard E Grant
Running time:16 minutes/colour
Date Completed: c.1987.

Film scripts

16   *The Judgment of Shylock.* In progress.

In fermentation/digestion

17   *The Inventors dilemma.* A novel?
18   *Five Fingers are not the same.* A novel?
19   *Turquoise.* A love story.
20   *The Weather of myself.* A philosophical book/diary.
21   *The Human Tragedy.* A true story, novel/poem?

Music

22   *I am here thank you please, a musical composition.* Contains an introduction on classical and romantic by orde.
Available 2014 as eBook and book (published by Song.
23   *Le Bordel Philosophique.* A musical composition with 5 contemporary composers (George

Barton, Sam Fernando, Cheryl Francis-Hoad, Simon Roth, Jaime Wolfson). A composition based on a poem, which is based on a painting to reach a musical gesamtkunstwerk for our era. Scheduled for completion 2014.

Plays

24   *Forcible Love.* A play based on the life of John Muafangejo.

25   *Forcible Love (NTN version).* A musical on the life of John Muafangejo - premiered at the National Theatre, Windhoek, Namibia for the Independence Celebrations. Includes reviews. Available 2014 as eBook and book (published by Song)

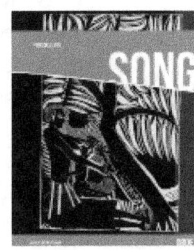

26   *The Rialto Dialogues.* Described as a revolutionary work about the Merchant of Venice by William Shakespeare. It includes the entire work uncut but introduces 4 new characters to open a meaning and channel to one of Shakespeare's greatest plays. Available 2014 as eBook and book (published by Song)

27   *Shylock the Magnificent.* A play 13 years after the Trial Scene of the Merchant of Venice by Shakespeare. Available 2014 as eBook and book (published by Song) See also The Soul's Heritage under poems.

Poems

28   *Miscellaneous poems.* Short poems found over the years. Available 2014 as eBook and book.

29   *The Love song of D. Adolph Hitler.* In progress.

30   *Der Tod Des Miguel.* In progress

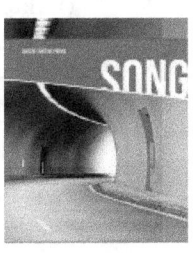

31   *Les Dem.* About Picasso's painting *Les Demoiselles D'Avignon*, includes essay on *Les Dem* by Professor Andrew Laird. Available 2014 as eBook and book (published by Song).

32   *Ndilapa Nkosi.* A lyrical comedy, first part of *The Soul's Heritage,* a trilogy, a landmark work described by Samuel Beckett as a 'moving feat'. Includes reviews and responses from various persons including Beckett.
Available 2014 as eBook and book (published by Song).

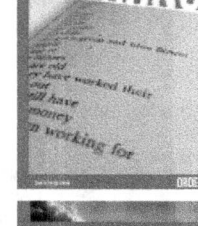

33   *Antomat Diplony of the Orb.* An epic comedy, in progress, second part of The Soul's Heritage, a trilogy.

34   *The Argonauta Vineyard.* A tragic comedy, in progress, third part of The Soul's Heritage, a trilogy.

35   *Parlez à Voir.*
Available 2014 as eBook and book (published by Song).

36   *Flying strongly on one wing.*
Available 2014 as eBook and book (published by Song).

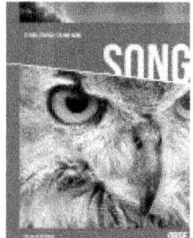

37   *Snowflakes and Ashes.*
Available 2014 as eBook and book (published by Song).

Reviews and articles

38   A number of articles and reviews exist and are being collated.

39   *Art, An Adaptive Function?*
Encyclopaedia of Evolution Mark Pagel (Editor-in-Chief), Oxford University Press, 2002. (365 articles from 330 different authors).

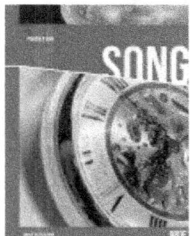

Visual works

Drawings, paintings, photography, prints, sculptures
Please see www.orde.info